| DATE | | | |
|------|---|---|---|
| 9.28.06 | | | |
| | | | |
| | | | |
| | | | |

633.645   Lasky, Kathryn 1021
LASK
          Sugaring time

(XII.)                              (9/91)

| DATE | BORROWER'S NAME | | |
|------|----------------|---|---|
| out 1-31-92 | BRYAN | Bryan W | K |
| 9.28.06 | Rahitha | | 2 |

1021

# SUGARING TIME

# SUGARING TIME

By KATHRYN LASKY

Photographs by
CHRISTOPHER G. KNIGHT

MACMILLAN PUBLISHING COMPANY ◆ NEW YORK

Macmillan Publishing Company
866 Third Avenue, New York, N.Y. 10022
Collier Macmillan Canada, Inc.
Printed in the United States of America
Designed by Leslie Bauman
10   9   8   7   6
Library of Congress Cataloging
in Publication Data
Lasky, Kathryn.
Sugaring time.
Summary: Text and photographs show how a
family taps the sap from maple trees and
processes it into maple syrup.
1. Maple sugar—Juvenile literature. 2. Maple
syrup—Juvenile literature. [1. Maple sugar.
2. Maple syrup] I. Knight, Christopher G., ill.
II. Title.
SB239.M3L37   1983      633.6′45      82-23928
ISBN 0-02-751680-6

For Meredith, who cares
–K.L. and C.G.K.

# ❖ A TIME OUT OF TIME ❖

There is a time between the seasons. It comes in March when winter seems tired and spring is only a hoped-for thing. The crystalline whiteness of February has vanished and there is not yet even the pale green stain in the trees that promises spring. It is a time out of time, when night, in central Vermont, can bring a fitful late winter storm that eases, the very next day, into sunshine and a melting wind from the southeast.

Many people complain about this time of year. Snow cannot be counted on for sledding or skiing; cars get stuck in muddy roads; clothes are mud-caked and hard to clean; and the old folks' arthritis kicks up. Everyone, young and old, gets cranky about staying indoors.

But for a few people, this time is a season in its own right. For them it is *sugaring time*, when the sap begins to flow in the maple grove or sugarbush, as it is called. It is a time that contradicts all farming calendars that say crops are planted in the spring, cared for in the summer, and harvested in the fall. This crop, maple sap, is harvested in March, and that is part of the specialness of sugaring time. It is special, too, because young people have a reason to go outside, snow or no snow, mud or no mud, and older people have a reason to believe in the coming spring.

Alice and Don Lacey and their three children live on a farm that has a small sugarbush. They have been waiting almost two weeks for the sap to start running. Last year they had started to hang buckets by town meeting time in early March. But this year's town meeting has come and gone by more than a week and the snow is still almost as high as the bellies of their Belgian workhorses, Jumping Jack and Tommy. It covers the meadow leading up to the sugarbush in a wind-packed, crusty blanket.

The Laceys wonder if the sap will get a jump on them this year. Before they can begin sugaring, they will have to spend a day or more using their horses to break out the trails to the sugarbush. And they cannot start breaking out until the days turn warm enough to loosen up the snow so the horses can get through it. The sap might be running for some time before they can get to the stand of maples covering the hillside at the top of the meadow. But there is no other way to get there.

By the end of the second week in March, however, the weather begins to change. The nights are still cold, below freezing, but one midmorning the thermometer is above freezing and still climbing. Icicles that have hung like scepters since December suddenly begin dripping like popsicles in August.

"It really feels like sugaring weather," Alice says.

"Tomorrow?" "Tomorrow?" "Tomorrow?" Jonathan, Angie, and Jeremy all ask their mother at once.

"Maybe," she replies. "If this holds. If it's cold tonight and warm again tomorrow, we'll be able to start breaking out, and then by the next day hang some buckets."

Tomorrow comes. It is warm but raining. Fog swirls through the valley and up into the meadow, covering the hills and mountaintops beyond. Everything is milky white. Snow-covered earth and sky melt together. Pines appear rootless, like ghost trees, their pointy tops wrapped in mist. It is a groundless world without edges or distances, a world that floats, private and cozy and detached, through the fog and clouds. There will be no breaking out today.

# ❖ BREAKING OUT ❖

Finally the day does come. A northwest wind blows the clouds and rain away, then quickly dies, and the sun shines until the mountaintops break through to a clear day. Snow is loosening up and the Laceys can almost hear the sap dripping in the sugarbush. Even a baby down in town was ready to get born and go! Don Lacey, who is a doctor, was up before the sun to deliver it.

Back home, Don harnesses up Tommy and Jumping Jack and walks behind them, urging them through the three-foot-deep snow. They are reluctant, even though there is no sled to pull on this first circuit. The snow is heavy, and their muscles are stiff.

Breaking out is the hardest part of sugaring. After three months of easy barn living with no loads to pull and not even a fly to swish away, the horses are winter lazy and stubborn. But the trails have to be broken if the trees are to be tapped and the sap gathered.

Don guides the horses toward the sugarhouse. Jonathan, who is eight, and Angie, six, follow on skis. The hoofprints that the horses leave are nearly a foot across and one and a half times as deep. With a sound like muffled thunder, their hoofs crush the snow.

This snow of early spring is called corn snow because the crystals are big and granular, like kernels of corn. But it is really more sugary in its texture, and when Jonathan skis it sounds as if he is skimming across the thick frosting of a wedding cake. He and Angie, on their skis, move faster than the horses across the snow, but at last the first loop to the sugarhouse and across the low ridge behind it is complete. Don turns the horses and circles back to the lower meadow. There, he and Alice hook the harnesses to a sturdy sled. They are going to cut out some runner marks on the trail.

Max, a young neighbor, has his first sled ride on Alice's lap as she skillfully guides the horses through the ups and downs and twists and turns of the half-broken trail that leads through the sugar maze. The horses are even more obstinate, now that they are pulling the sled. They balk at a muddy trickle of a creek, they stop on the incline of a curve. They are like two stubborn babies—each weighing nearly a ton. But Alice is firm. She scolds and cajoles them through the heavy snow and gradually coaxes the winter laziness out of their bones. Two hours later the first trail is completely broken out. Tomorrow, they will go for the higher ones.

The next day is warmer still. The meadow is scored with dozens of small rivulets of melting snow, and the road and lower paths are muddy. Streams that have lain as still as black ribbons in the snow now rush, muddy and raucous, down the hills. The world slips and slides in the thick mud. Early this morning, a car slid into a ditch down the road, and another one followed while trying to get the first one out. Then a neighbor's dog got into the Laceys' sheep yard, barked, chased around, raised havoc, and scared the wits out of a pregnant ewe, who in her panic skidded headfirst into the creek. Alice came out when she heard the commotion and rescued the ewe. It is late morning by the time the horses are hitched up. But breaking out is easier this time and goes much faster.

# ⇥⬥⇤ TAPPING TIME ⇥⬥⇤

The big trails have been broken out. Another cold spell comes, giving the Laceys just enough time to get the tapholes drilled into the maple trees and the buckets hung before the sap starts rising again.

They load up the sled with buckets and lids, called hats, and spouts. In all, nearly two hundred holes will be drilled, two hundred spouts hammered into the holes, and two hundred buckets hung. Alice fetches the drill and bit. When the sled is stacked with buckets, spouts, and hats, there is room only for Alice and two small children, not medium-sized, but really small children, who would get stuck in the deep drifts of snow if they were not snug in the sled. So Jeremy and Max are packed aboard with the sugaring tools, while Don, Jonathan, and Angie strap on their skis.

The runners glide over the freshly broken trails. It is a cold, windless day. The sky is clear, and in the deep silence of the woods one bird can be heard singing. The trees stand waiting, ready to give up some of the clear sap that circulates just beneath the bark. Alice and Don will drill carefully. Often, more than one hole is drilled in a tree, especially if it is a good running tree. But they will not go too deep or drill too many holes at a time in one tree. They mean to take only a little of each tree's sap, for that is its source of vitality, its nourishment, its life.

The sugar sap is made in the tree primarily for its own use, not for people's use. It helps the tree to live and grow. Sunlight and warmth start the sugar-making activity beneath the surface of the tree.

Some people, especially a long time ago, gashed maple trees with an ax or chopped big notches into their trunks. Like gaping wounds, these cuts would pour forth the sap, but they would never heal and within a few years the sugar maples would die.

Alice and Don begin to drill. The bit, or pointed part of the drill, is just under one-half inch in diameter and the holes are no more than one and one-half inches deep. The holes are slanted upward into the tree to catch the sap, for although the saying is "Sap's rising!," the movement of the sap within the tree is downward as well as upward, around about, and every which way. Last year, Jonathan hammered in the spouts; this year he will do that again and help with the drilling, too.

Angie is now tall enough to reach up and put the hats on the buckets to keep out the rain and snow. Jeremy, three, and Max, four, still too small to walk a long way in the big drifts, will hand her the hats from the sled.

Seventy-five buckets have been hung by the end of this first day. Alice has steered the huge Belgians and her sledful of spouts and buckets and children through the twists and turns and dips and rises of the sugar maze without spilling a child or a hat.

# "SAP'S RISING!"

The buckets have hung for over three days but the weather has not been the kind that makes for a real flow of sap. It has been below freezing, day and night, with thick cloud cover. No sun, no warmth, no flow. Standing in the sugarbush, you can hear the creaking of maples as the cold wind blows in from Canada.

Finally, after a freezing cold night, the next morning is sunny. It is not the pale, thin, low-angle sunlight of November, but the direct, strengthening light of a sun that has passed the year's equator, the vernal equinox. It is the sun of longer days that feels warm on the cheeks, makes birds sing, and helps all things loosen up and stretch.

The frost designs on Jonathan's bedroom window have melted before he has dressed this morning. Bright lances of sunlight do a crazy crisscross dance on Angie's covers if she wiggles her knees. Little Jeremy climbs up on a stool by his window and takes a quiet look at the sunlit world outside.

"Sap's rising!" Alice calls up. "It's going to flow today!"

The sap flows all day, not in little drips or plinks, but in what Jonathan calls long "drrriiips." It is the sweet maple song of spring to Jonathan's and Angie's ears as they stand in the sugarbush. By tomorrow, they tell each other, the buckets will be full enough to gather. Angie and Jonathan lift the hats and peek into the buckets. The sparkling sap, clear and bright, runs like streams of Christmas tinsel. They each take a lick and wonder how so much crystal sweetness can come from a gnarled tree older than all their grandparents put together.

And it will flow, because sunlight is the energy for the tree's sugar-making process. Last year, sunlight from the sky, carbon dioxide from the air, and chlorophyll in the green leaves worked together to make the sugar that nourishes the tree. All winter, the sugar has been stored in the bark and wood of roots and stems. Long before the first leaf is seen, watery sap carrying the sugar begins to stir under the bark, reviving the tree for a new cycle of growth.

Betty Brown, Alice's mother and the children's grandmother, arrives every year at almost precisely the time when the sap starts to flow. She comes from far away, but somehow she seems to know just when the sap will move and she likes to be there. She likes the notion of things flowing and giving up their sweetness after months of winterlock. She likes to know that spring is coming even if you cannot see a touch of green or hear a robin.

Alice and Don hitch up the horses for the first gathering run and Betty heads for the sugarhouse to wash out the pans of the evaporator in which the sap will be boiled. This time the trip along the sugar trail is different. The sides of the sled have been removed and the huge round gathering tank is set on top of it. The sounds are different too, as Tommy and Jumping Jack pull the sled over mud and the crust of the snow, which is thin and wet. No longer do the runners make a sugary whisper over the granular corn snow of three weeks ago. Now there are damp sucks and squishes, the sound of mud and fast-melting snow, and the wet crunch of last year's leaves under the runners. It is harder to drive the team now than when the trails were slick with packed snow. Alice braces Jeremy between her legs and the tank. Jonathan rides the corner of the sled bracing Max.

They stop at the first stand of maples. Jonathan removes a hat from a bucket. It is brim-full, and a world is mirrored in its crystalline surface. Bark shimmers, branches quiver, a whole sky with clouds and sunbursts is reflected in the tree's sweet water. It is a bucketful of life that Jonathan cannot resist. He dips a jar into the sap for the first real taste of spring, and then begins gathering. He and Angie and their father pour the contents of the tree buckets into the gathering bucket. This special container has a flared rim, so the sap will not slosh over as it is carried to the gathering tank on the sled. It is heavy work. One full gathering bucket can weigh nearly thirty pounds. Jonathan can almost carry a full bucket, but Angie tries for one that is only a third full.

As the sap is poured into the gathering tank on the sled, a cone-shaped metal filter set inside the tank strains out any bark and leaves that have dropped into the tree buckets. This is the first of three filterings in the syrup-making process.

The gathering tank holds four barrels, or 128 gallons. It is huge, at least from Jeremy's and Max's point of view. They ride along, holding onto its rim, peering down into the hollow darkness and listening to the sloshes in the tank. Max and Jeremy yell "Hoo! Hoo!," making their own scary echoes in the dark drum.

They make many loops through the sugarbush. The load becomes heavier as the tank fills up, and the horses go more slowly. Alice lets the horses stop to drink cool sweet sap from the hanging buckets. Then she turns the team toward the sugarhouse.

Alice stops the horses on a bank just above the storage tank against the back wall of the sugarhouse. A pipe on the gathering tank sends a river of sap running downhill through a gutter to the storage tank. The children take quick sips from the fast-moving current.

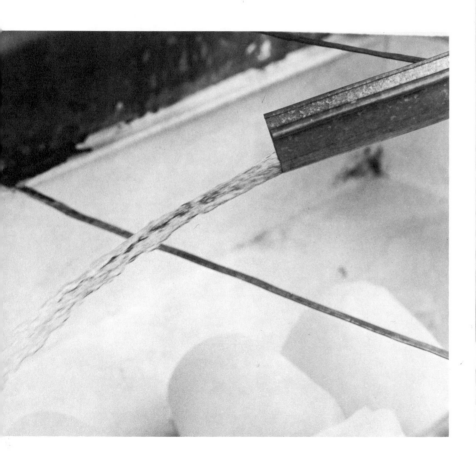

# ❖ BOILING ❖

For two days, a southeast wind has brought spring rain to melt the snow and unlock the frozen earth from its winter prison. There are ragged snow patches scattered here and there on the meadow like torn remnants of the white blanket that covered it for nearly four months. The trees have nearly finished their run. The sap has all been gathered and waits in the storage tank behind the sugarhouse. It must be boiled within a week or it may spoil. Forty gallons of sap will become only one gallon of syrup, so it is inefficient to boil small quantities. Now that the tank is full, boiling can begin.

One morning, the melting, earthy smell of spring up in the meadow suddenly turns sweet a few hundred feet from the sugarhouse. Steam rolls out the open ends of the house and smoke rises from the chimney in back. Being inside is like sitting in a maple cloud surrounded by the muffled roar of the fire and the bubbling tumble of boiling sap. Betty Brown and the children are there, their cheeks wet and shiny in the mapley mist. This is their first celebration, except birthdays, since Christmas. Boiling time is like a party, a party that celebrates mud and greenness, sweetness and renewed life.

Alice scoops up cups of boiling sap and steeps tea bags in them for sap tea. The children drink it while sitting on logs, using upside-down buckets as tea tables. After they finish, Betty leans on her walking stick listening to the thrum of the fire and the wild din of her grandson Jeremy and his friend Max beating a raucous sugar song on the upturned buckets.

Early this morning, Alice and Don started the fire in the arch, the firebox beneath the boiling pans. They have at least fifteen hours of boiling ahead, all day and part of the night. People will come and go and watch and sniff and talk and taste. Some people even come up to the sugarhouse to clear a spring cold. There's nothing like the mapley steam for that. Children stay up later than usual, and supper is not at the regular time or at the regular place, but catch as catch can up in the sugarhouse.

Sap flows into the evaporator pans by gravity through a pipe from the storage tank. Sugarhouses are often built against hillsides to take advantage of this downhill flow. A float valve regulates the amount of sap that flows into the pans so they won't overflow. More is allowed in automatically as water is evaporated.

The two pans of the evaporator are about four feet long, three feet wide, and one foot deep. They are positioned end to end over the fire in the arch. The first pan is partitioned lengthwise down the center into two parts. The second has four sections partitioned over the hottest part of the fire. The sap is channeled through these various partitions toward a spigot at the end of the fourth partition in the second pan where syrup is drawn off. The constant feed of fresh sap into the pans pushes the sap which has boiled the longest toward this drain-off point.

Tending the boiling sap is busy work. Someone always has to be on his or her feet, either skimming the sap, stoking the fire, or testing the temperature. Jonathan is now tall enough and careful enough to stand by the rim of the pans and help Alice skim off the foam from the hot sap with the long-handled skimmer.

The foam is a natural way in which the sap cleanses itself of foreign matter, such as bits of bark and *niter,* a kind of salt sometimes called "sugar sand" which rises to the top when the sap is boiled. The skimmer has a sieve bottom. After each dip, either Jonathan or Alice flings the foam out through a small window set conveniently by the first pan. Sometimes, however, a wild surge of foam can turn the pans into tumultuous oceans of bubbles. To avoid a boil-over, Alice tosses in a dab of butter. This calms the boiling by breaking the surface tension, just as oil on stormy waters helps anxious sailors in a gale.

Angie, though not quite tall enough to skim, is just the right size to help keep the hungry fires in the arch going by handing wood to her father through the small door that connects the woodshed to the sugarhouse. And Jeremy, lulled by the bubbling tumble of the boiling sap, is just the right size to fall asleep in his grandma's arms.

Outside, the wind freshens, the sky grows bluer, and puffy white clouds sail over the ridge. But inside the sugarhouse it is different weather. The maple fog grows thicker. There are a few slivers and slats of light from the cracks between the boards of the walls. The fire thrums in the arch, and while Jeremy sleeps the others become more watchful for the telltale signs of sap turning to syrup. They must be alert now, for the temperature of the sap is rising. Sap turns to syrup at 218 degrees Fahrenheit. Things can move fast, too fast. The sap can turn to syrup, then to cream, within a few seconds and a few degrees, then burn in the pans. Hot syrup burns rapidly and can even explode.

Jonathan and his father are dipping the thermometer in frequently now as the temperature rises. There are other signs that the sap is about to turn. It becomes darker, taking on a golden amber tone. The bubbles look different, too. Near the end, just before the sap turns to syrup, the bubbles become very fine, then suddenly grow quite huge and explosive

looking. And finally, when the liquid "aprons" or "sheets," the Laceys know that it is syrup. They use a tool similar to the skimmer to test for sheeting. If the liquid drops off in rapid little droplets it is not sheeting, but if it gathers along the edge of the scoop slowly and does not immediately dribble off in separate drops, then it is said to sheet. Only syrup sheets, not sap.

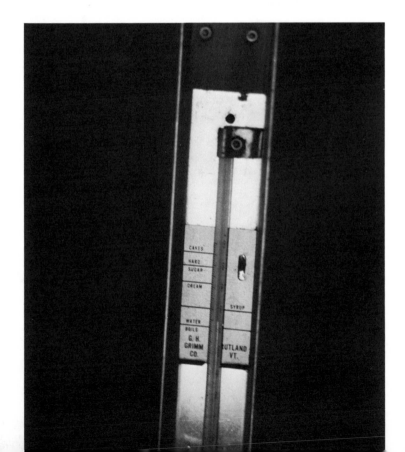

"Two hundred fifteen degrees, Dad," Jonathan says, and two minutes later, "Two hundred sixteen, Dad," and then, "Two hundred eighteen!"

"Is it sheeting?" Alice asks.

"Not quite," says Don. "Let's let it go to 219."

In another minute, Don exclaims, "We've got syrup!" Cheers rise in the maple fog. "We're ready to draw off."

They place a bucket under the drain-off spigot and a golden stream begins to run.

In this first drawing off there are nearly three gallons of syrup. They all work quickly now. Jonathan fetches the hydrometer, an instrument for checking the specific gravity, or density, of the liquid. Syrup should weigh eleven pounds per gallon. This is the weight at which it keeps best. If it is too heavy, it may crystallize; if it is too thin, it may ferment. The hydrometer will float at the red line marked 31.5 if the syrup is the proper weight. When the 31.5 mark sinks below the surface, they close the spigot and wait for more sap to turn to syrup.

"Clear the way! Hot syrup!"

Max and Jeremy back away. Being scalded by syrup could be a real disaster. Don carries the bucket to the filtering tank, where he pours it through felt funnels lined with heavy paper. This is the final step in cleansing the syrup and making sure it is crystal clear. The solid matter has been skimmed off, but traces of niter can remain. Filtering strains out these traces.

"When can we taste? When can we taste?" the children ask.

Don measures out a small cup of syrup for each child and puts them on a shelf to cool. "No drinking yet," he warns. "You'll burn your tongues."

When the cups have cooled and the children have tasted the first sap there are immediate cries for "More! More! More!"

Don takes some of the syrup and puts it into a small glass jar for grading. There are three grades of Vermont maple syrup. They are called Fancy, Grade A, and Grade B. Fancy is the purest, just barely amber. Grade A is light amber and more mapley in taste, and Grade B is darker with an even stronger flavor. In the old days, one hundred years ago or more, people in the Northeast used maple sugar intead of cane sugar because it was cheaper and more easily available. They wanted the maple sweetener to be as much like cane sugar as possible. This meant it should be white or as nearly colorless as possible, sweet but unmapley or mild in flavor. Maple-tasting coffee was not their goal. That system worked fine one hundred years ago when Fancy meant best and best meant most like cane sugar. But today, the system is not so sensible, especially for people who want a real maple flavor. To their taste the best maple syrup is not always Fancy. Many of these people will buy Grade A instead.

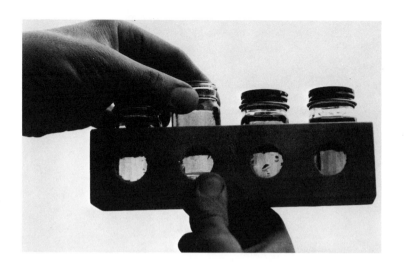

will burn in the sugarhouse. The only light in the house will be the fiery orange glow through the grate of the arch. But that is not enough light to read by and there is no bed to sleep on, no radio to listen to. At night in the sugarhouse, a person can only think and dream and tend the arch. But it doesn't matter, for it is a gentle darkness that smells like maple clouds and reminds you of a winter now gone and a spring just born.

A grading set consists of sample jars of Fancy, Grade A, and Grade B. When Don Lacey grades the family's own syrup and it is lighter than the Fancy sample, it may be called Fancy. If, however, it is not so light as Fancy but lighter than Grade A, it may be called A. If it is darker than A but lighter than Grade B it may be called B.

The children drink the syrup slowly from their cups. Soon they will have their sandwich dinner and go down the darkening meadow to bed, but Don will stay on until close to midnight. Through the starless night the fires

# ⊶ THE SWEET TASTE ⊷

On a windless, starry night, it started again, coming down softly, almost secretly, and covering everything with its sparkling whiteness on Easter eve. It is an April snowfall, the very last snowfall of the season. The children are thrilled, for it means a sugar-on-snow party with the new maple syrup. The cold sweet taste is much better than jelly beans or even chocolate Easter eggs. Alice boils the syrup until it is foamy and slightly thicker. Then the children race with the pan of warm syrup to the meadow's corner, followed by Alice, carrying cider and doughnuts. They smooth and pack a place in the small patch of snow and pour the syrup, sometimes dribbling it in designs that look like twisting rivers or sometimes pooling it into golden puddles.

Within a few seconds it grows cold and waxy and chewy. They twist it around forks or pick it up with their fingers and eat it. They drink the last of the year's cider with the first of the year's syrup and eat powdered doughnuts. This is the second taste of the new maple syrup. The first was a pancake breakfast, the morning after the boiling.

"Is it sweeter than last year's?" someone asked at that breakfast.

"Yes, and less woody."

"More smoky, but clear."

"No Fancy, but Grade A is as mild as the last Fancy of last year, and B is much sweeter than it has been for four years."

The talk at the breakfast table was all about sweetness and clarity and color. Stories were told of old-timers who could tell by taste which stand of maples within a county a jug of syrup came from. They could tell by taste whether the sugarbush was in a valley or on a hillside facing south, whether the trees were young or old.

Later on in the year, perhaps around Halloween and certainly in time for Christmas, Alice will get out the molds—the maple leaf ones, or hearts, or the alphabet. She and the children will make some maple sugar candy.

Within four weeks it is all over. The shortest season of all is finished. The sap has stopped running, but its sweet syrup will be tasted throughout the rest of the year: There will be pancake breakfasts almost weekly, maple candy for trick or treat at Halloween, gifts at Christmas, and more sugar-on-snow parties in the winter to come, when the whole meadow lies under a blanket of snow for months and months.

# ·⋅·✦·⋅· A SEASON BY ·⋅·✦·⋅·

Sugaring time has been over for more than two months. A crop has been harvested but the plant is still living and growing. The meadow is dotted with daisies and Indian paintbrush and wild strawberries. Alice and the children bring all the buckets and hats and spouts down from the sugarhouse, and scour them with washing soda on the front lawn in the hot June sun.

The longest day of the year is approaching. It has been coming since the vernal equinox in March when the sun began to grow stronger. After midsummer night, the days will grow shorter by seconds, then the seconds will collect into minutes, and the minutes into hours. But throughout the summer, the trees will grow leafier and greener because of the sap that began circulating under the bark and nourishing the tree in March. In July, new buds will form; from them new leaves will grow next year.

Sometimes it is easy to think of darkness on the brightest summer day, or November in June, and now, when the seconds begin to vanish from the daylight, there can be fleeting thoughts of winter. It is impossible to stay a summer against a winter, to make it last forever. But there is a comfort in knowing, in the warm, slowly vanishing light of summer, that deep in the roots and just under the bark, the green trees are quietly making sap and storing it for that time out of time, that sugaring time, when winter seems tired and spring is only a hoped-for thing.

‒❊‒